JOY
INTERRUPTED

Geoffrey Lilburne offers a powerful account of living with depression and the reclaiming of joy. Blending historical developments of chemical theories and treatments for depression with his existential and spiritual journey, he offers readers an intimacy with sadness, doubt, tenacity and devotion. His openhearted spirit of inquiry is challenging, revealed through many poignant stories of distressing times. Yet what shines through is Geof's willingness to honour the fullness of his life as lived, to see beyond the obvious, to retrieve what despair could have him forget, and to go towards the future with trust and faith. Along the way he enriches his understandings of prayer, devotion, God and spirituality. He acknowledges the significance of fulfilling work, creative and enriching interpersonal relationships and supportive communities in the return to joy. Moving and poetic.

Dr Ian Percy, Family Therapist, Perth

Mental illness is no longer the taboo it once was, but an awareness – and often an acknowledgment – of how debilitating and destructive it can be can still not be assumed. We need to hear the stories of those who have suffered its horrors. This is perhaps as true in the church as in any other domain of contemporary culture. Geof Lilburne has provided one such story – a deeply revealing, searingly honest account of his experience of depression and his attempts to negotiate his way through it within the context of Christian faith. With his theologian's wisdom and an academic's critical skills, he provides us with a particular combination of insights into the nature of depression. He offers a perspective on the strengths and weaknesses of the ways it been medicalised and treated. He opens horizons on how faith and prayer weave their way in and out of the life of the mentally ill Christian. This book will resonate as much with those who have suffered depression as with those who have journeyed with them in their suffering. It is also a book that those who have no acquaintance with depression would do well to read. It would be another small step in breaking down the ignorance of the realities of depression. I'm sure that all who read it will be grateful that Geof has written it.

Dr Geoff Thompson, Co-ordinator of Studies, Systematic Theology, Pilgrim Theological College

Pills or prayers? Geoffrey Lilburne, minister and educator, offers his extended reflection on the experiences of depression; and shares his experiences of a lifetime of living with a mood disorder. He calls for a holistic approach that involves not only medical science but serious engagement with a person's faith journey. This memoir may encourage others to tell their stories as well as help people to respond with sensitivity and encouragement.

Dr Nancy Ault, Senior Lecturer in Practical Theology, Murdoch University.

JOY
INTERRUPTED

A MEMOIR
OF DEPRESSION AND
PRAYER

GEOFFREY LILBURNE

COVENTRY
PRESS

Published in Australia by
Coventry Press
33 Scoresby Road
Bayswater Vic. 3153
Australia

First published by Coventry Press in 2018.

ISBN 9780648145769

Cataloguing-in-Publication entry is available from the National Library of Australia http:/catalogue.nla.gov.au/.

Text design by Filmshot Graphics (FSG)
Cover design by Ian James – www.jgd.com.au

Printed in Australia

Contents

PROLOGUE

I stood on the banks of the Murrumbidgee River. It's today or never, I concluded. If I don't take the plunge today, I'll probably never again be given the opportunity. But the current seemed strong, and the water was cold on my bare toes. Looking across the other side, I could see a beautiful waterfall playing over the rocks, and the suggestion of deep rock pools, higher up the hill side. I waded out into the water. I could feel the strength of the current now. The stream quickly got much deeper. I came back and reconsidered. Then I broke off a long stick, I waded out a second time, checking the depth of the water in front of me. I was nearly swept off my feet in the downward sloping bottom, nearly lost my stick and dropped my shoes in the water. Back again...

Would I push myself into the powerful cold current or would I stay safe on the shore? Would I take the plunge I had dreamed of making or stay with my sadness on this side of the great divide? I had come to this turning point after a life-time in education and ministry, a life-time during which I had battled unceasingly with a dark marauder of life, clinical depression. This is my story of how depression shaped my life, and how, in the fullness of time, I was delivered by joy.

1: DARKNESS

OVERWHELMED BY SADNESS

I awoke one morning wishing that I had died during the night. The evening before, I had sobbed myself to sleep and simply longed for the darkness to cover me. The approach of day filled me with dread, and I clung to my bed in a futile attempt to avoid the inevitable. My parents called me from the kitchen, "Time for breakfast, lad. Come on, get lively. School today!" I was thirteen years of age.

School! For the first time in my life, I hated school. School seemed like a bleak prison where I was forced to undergo trials beyond my capacity. Not that I was a poor student. In fact, quite the opposite. The school was the first in Western Australia of an old style of selective schools, which creamed off the best performers from around the city and placed them in one of four classes, two for girls and two for boys. And among this select company, I was one of the best students, usually coming near the top of the group in the regular term exams. What then was the problem? It was more in the play-ground than in the class room. It was not that I was even unpopular or singled out for bullying. Rather, it was my sense of intense discomfort around my fellow students. I felt like I didn't fit. I was out of place.

After more than sixty years, it's easy to come up with explanations. At the time, I had no explanation. I didn't even have words for what I was feeling. It seemed to me that all the colour had been drained out of my life, that what had hitherto been a rich and exciting adventure had now been reduced to a black and white ordeal, all of which caused me distress. I knew something was wrong, terribly wrong, but what it was I had no idea. The worst was to think that someone else might find out about this affliction, and that severe consequences would follow.[1]

Immediately prior to this descent into darkness, I had taken a term holiday in the South-West, staying in a sea-side town with a couple of cousins and my aunt and uncle. My cousin of the same age was already exploring the oceans around the town and had joined up with some professional fishers to further his interest. He had no time for me, but my Uncle Greg had recently purchased a small block of virgin land, and he was intent on spending his vacation working there. I fitted his plans, especially when he saw that I could be trained to drive a tractor. I spent the week atop an ancient machine, hauling an equally ancient seed drill around the wind-rowed strips of land, seeding oats with super-phosphate.

I was in heaven, exploring some newly acquired manhood in the seat of this tractor, and playing my part in this grand project of land settlement. Each morning, Uncle and I were up early, filled up the tanks with petrol and drove twenty kilometres to the "block", where the tractor was fuelled, the seed drill loaded, and I took off across the roughly leveled ground, on a mission of transformation. My senses were on fire, I loved the smell of the super fertiliser, even the sting of the petrol as we fuelled up, filled with anticipation. I loved every moment of it, and soon formed the plan in mind to persuade my father to purchase just such a block, just such a tractor and drill, and begin a similar project in the Perth hills.

I don't recall the conversation on my return to the city, but I do recall Dad's words of rebuke to me: "Don't be ridiculous!" The plan that seemed so foolproof to me was derided as a sure way to lose money and waste time. The next day was Monday, and it was back to school. Sometime during this week back, the sudden disconcerting mood swing set in.[2] I dragged myself to school and longed for the hours of retreat into sleep.

I should say more about this school experience. We were a feisty bunch of young lads, all showing some early signs of academic promise. I loved my first year at the school in which I'd been assigned to class 1B, along with all boys whose names occupied the second half of the alphabet. In our class, we had some that liked science and a larger group who liked poetry and the arts. A few of us showed sporting prowess, but nothing amazing in that department. My small stature and lack of hand-eye coordination did not seem to be a huge disadvantage among this jolly group of lads. I didn't belong to any of the more defined groups, but seemed to get along with all my fellows and perhaps looked forward to growing some friendships in my second year like I'd known at Primary School.

All that changed in my second year. For some reason, the class sizes were unequal, and it was decided that one lad should be moved from the 1B group over into the 1A group, now suitably transformed into 2F. I was the lucky chap, as my name began with an L and I therefore had the lowest alphabetical score in the class. So, without discussion, consultation, or any explanation, I was simply told in the first day back that henceforth I would be a member of the other group of boys. An apparently important administrative anomaly had been deftly solved, and I was the unwitting solution.

2F presented quite a different group of boys that I must now get to know. I don't think anyone in this group liked poetry — sport seemed to be the joining force here — and the boys seemed bigger than me and I guess more advanced in physical development. Although I had heard about sex and orgasm the year before among my 1B mates, it seemed too that this group had more "runs on the board" than me when it came to sexual experience. It was clear – I didn't belong. I went home and sobbed myself to sleep that first night.

Of course, there was no alternative but to "soldier on", which is what I did. So, when at the end of first term, there came the opportunity to have a holiday in the south coast, I was up for it! I had no idea what vistas would open up for me, until Uncle Greg asked me if I would like to help him with his farm. After my school experience, I now felt liberated and elevated all at once. I loved the work, loved working with my uncle, felt, perhaps for the first time, that I was becoming a man. It was such a heady mix that I couldn't wait to get home and explain my great plan to my father.

I was completely nonplussed by his reaction, and soon after, the descent into darkness occurred for me. I'd always been a sensitive child, and I often discovered that the period of return from holiday effected some kind of sadness in me. I would wish I was still at the enjoyable exotic place and would find my present situation dull in comparison. But on this occasion, the contrast between the high of the vacation with my uncle driving his tractor and the drabness of my life as an out-of-place school boy seemed to push me over some kind of precipice.

My parents were modest people and we were by no means wealthy. But it seemed entirely reasonable to me that my father could find the means to purchase a small property. If my uncle could do it, why not my father? However, it was the situation at school that probably tipped the balance. Feeling so out of place and awkward in the presence of my peers pitched me into a dark and lonely place. Each day, I longed for the day to be over and the night to come. I would retreat to my bed and feel I had reached the best part of the day. As I fell asleep, I hoped that the darkness would cover me forever, only to find the dawn breaking and the burden of another day thrust upon me.[3]

Of course, the problem was made worse for me in that I had no idea of what was happening. I could not understand why my life suddenly seemed so burdensome. Being a conscientious child, I determined just to pretend nothing was wrong and to carry on as best I could. The worst thing I could do, or so it seemed to me, was to let on to anyone what was happening to me. My bedroom was far from my parent's room, so they probably did not hear my nightly sobbing.

I remember one teacher approaching me one day in the play-ground with the question: "Is anything wrong, Geoff? You don't seem to be yourself lately". My mumbled reply, as I recall, was along the lines, "Oh no, sir, nothing is wrong". Today I bless that man and wish I had been able to tell him what his kind intervention meant to me. But for all intents and purposes, I was lost, without any support or solace, lost in my own overwhelming sadness and isolation.

Of course, nothing lasts forever, and after a couple of weeks, the darkness began to lift and I felt that life wasn't really so bad. I still wanted Dad to buy a farm, and I still felt miserable at school, but there were parts of life, especially my weekends, which seemed to offer some joy, so my spirits lifted. But something had changed forever. I dreaded the return of the darkness, and I knew that if this could happen to me so suddenly without reason, there was no telling when it might return. My confidence — in life and in myself — was broken, and I somehow lost the childhood capacity for careless enjoyment.

In retrospect, it seems to me that I left the world of childhood and suddenly became a kind of adult, serious about the world, my place in it, and the duties I should henceforth undertake. With this new seriousness, I began to feel that it was very important that I measured my life against others, just to make sure that I was "measuring up" and was, after all, "normal". I continued to love my parents and to work hard at school. I don't remember having much fun.

Life as a school-boy in the 1950s wasn't meant to be fun, so I continued to do my best. My hopes and dreams were deflected into the future, and I began to search the "land for sale" columns in weekend papers and introduce to my father suitable blocks that were being opened up at Chidlow and Gidgegannup in the hills east of Perth. I sought to persuade him that these blocks were affordable and would indeed constitute a "good investment". He agreed that occasionally on a weekend drive we could pass one or other of these blocks, but, of course, no visits were arranged and no purchase made. I remember the song of Slim Dusty, "The Pub with No Beer" and its mention of the loneliness of the campfire evoked in me a kind of nostalgia for a life I had never known.

At the time of this experience, I had no idea about prayer. My wordless wishes directed at the darkness could hardly be characterised as a kind of prayer, because they were more in the nature of a longing than anything that could be voiced. But even if prayer had come into my mind, would it really have helped me in the struggle I was engaged? The idea would have been swiftly dismissed, because prayer involves a kind of hope or faith that there is a way out of this, and it was precisely this hope which my feelings denied.[4] This was my natural state of belief, before, that is, I encountered a different and rather challenging kind of Christianity.

A RELIGIOUS RESPONSE?

The story of my conversion to Christian faith may seem at first to be unrelated to the preceding narrative. But it will be the proposal of this book that there are a number of deep and informative connections between the first set of experiences and those that I now relate. In the year following my descent into darkness, my parents began to impress upon me the need to develop a social life outside the home. In response, I joined a boys Christian group meeting in the home of a local leader.

Naturally enough, I dreaded these evenings, not because of the religious teaching which was on offer, but because of my extreme discomfort in social settings with my peers. It seemed to be just like what I was experiencing in school, and I found myself unable to relax and enjoy the games and socialising that made up the evenings. I would have preferred to have stayed home with my parents, my model aircraft, or my crystal set! The early part of my weekend was regularly spoiled by a build-up of anxiety as Saturday night approached. Only Sunday morning and a day at home offered sweet relief. I decided I was an odd sort of person, because no one else seemed to be suffering in the way I was. I think I already traced this back to the experience of the year before when darkness descended.

It now seems strange that I persisted in attending this group. But, conscientious to a fault, I realised that socialising was an important element of life, even though I found it painful. Despite the fact that the social side of the event — which was meant to make it attractive to boys my age — repelled me, I was drawn to the more serious side of the evening and found my interest was richly rewarded by the leaders of the group. These leaders — and one in particular — provided a kind of older male model to me, and their offer of friendship and support was gladly accepted. In this way, I was drawn into a rather intense form of Christian discipleship, which seemed to offer an answer to many of the personal dilemmas I was facing.

The Christianity in which I was being encouraged spoke sternly of sin and the need for purity. Among other things, this involved a prohibition of masturbation, a favourite pastime of boys my age. Also of great importance was the "witness" to Christ that one offered to one's peers. When leaders spoke of the "cost of discipleship" I was sure that this was it—courting scorn and unpopularity by identifying as a Christian among other, carefree lads. This challenging and confronting form of Christianity had a deep appeal to me for I felt that much was amiss in my life. It offered a way to make things better and even to give a reason for the unpopularity I felt. It was sharply distinguished from the kind of Christianity to which my parents adhered. Their religion was not much more than Sunday observance, while this spoke of a commitment of personal life and a clear identification of the self with the claims of Jesus Christ. In my newfound seriousness, I soon began to feel that something was required of me if I were to respond to the claims of Christ and find my salvation. Leaders were eager to guide me into this way, and after attending several camps away in the hills, I came to the momentous decision to "give my life to Christ".

I recall quite vividly the warm glow in my heart as I returned to my camp bed after the decisive session with a leader. A new light had entered my life, and I felt that nothing would henceforth be the same. It was already twelve months since the dark episode, and it seemed my life had now taken a new direction which would steer me in the direction of the light rather than of the darkness. Prayer now became a regular feature of my life, thanking God for divine goodness and praying my way through lists of good causes and needy persons.

From this point on, my life took many new turns. The dark experience did not occupy my thoughts, but a certain vulnerability had been inserted into my life by my early experience. The careless joys of childhood were replaced by a more considered approach to my life and an overweening self-consciousness and awareness. All this was taken into the mix with my new found religious faith. A few years later, I began to keep a journal, that recorded in precise terms the results of my introspection and prayer. Often, I was "convicted of my sinfulness" and turned in new hope to God for a fresh start.

Prayerfulness now marked my life and the upsets of my early adolescence seemed far away. But would this life of prayer offer a lasting antidote to the experience of intense sadness, and how would I respond if such an experience recurred for me? These questions did not surface at this point, but it was not long before unfolding events made them once again urgent issues for consideration. In my next chapter, we will see how the intertwining of prayer and depression provide further occasion for reflection.

2: INSIGHT

The events of my thirteenth and fourteenth years had a profound effect on the remainder of my high school years. My innocent confidence in myself and in life had been shattered, and henceforth I lived my life with a certain sense of burden, the weight of my own loss of simple joy and the challenge to be a good disciple of Christ. To say I was a serious young man is to put it mildly, and I was sometimes teased by uncles and cousins for my new-found demeanour. What I had discovered, however, was a pattern of stability. Secure in my family home, I rested often in the love of parents and the intimacy of the family bonds. Nothing changed there.

But in addition to the stable home, I had now entered a close-knit Christian fellowship of like-minded young men where I could develop my skills in friendship and leadership. This was an important training ground for my later careers in high school teaching and Christian ministry. The group allowed little variation of thought or practice, but it provided a transition group to move me gently beyond the home sphere and into the world, or at least, a selected slice of the world. Given these two important supports to my life, the kind of psychological disturbance I had experienced so rudely as a 13-year-old did not recur. It was only as one or the other of these shifted that I would experience further psychological distress. What was gone from my experience, seemingly forever, was the joy of living. And that, perhaps, makes a good beginning definition of depression — the simple loss of joy.

Given the security I had developed, however, my self-confidence gradually returned and I was able to complete my high school years with a successful outcome of my matriculation examinations. I scored very high results and it was taken for granted that I would proceed to university studies. The only issue was choosing the course in which to enrol. In response to my religious and emotional experience, I resolved to undertake studies that would relate me to the human community rather than to scientific research, and I decided to train to become a school teacher. During my years of university study, I learned many new languages, and that of psychological analysis and theory was one of them. However, my majors in Anthropology and History kept me well away from any intense engagement with psychology or reflection on my own early experiences.

A PATTERN EMERGES

During my third year, I experienced a second major psychological disturbance that manifested in what I can now only describe as a form of extreme mental exhaustion and mania. I had moved out of home and taken up residence in a new university college, when towards the end of the year, I found myself quite unable to concentrate on my studies. I found myself in an unusually sociable manner of living; and sitting quietly and concentrating was quite beyond my capability.

The year had been one of super stimulus. Living away from home opened up opportunities for social engagement and I was active in the life of the college and university, in sporting and religious groups. As the end of year loomed, the writing of lengthy essays and cramming for examinations proved quite beyond my capability. I was too restless to sit still for long, and preferred the company of others to the quiet discipline of academic concentration. It appeared to me that I was headed for failure in the final year of my Bachelor of Arts, and this would be catastrophic for my career plans and quite outside my normal experience.

It did not occur to me to discuss the difficulties with anyone else: what was imperative was that I come up with a plan to avoid disaster. I resolved that I should seek a deferral of my exams and take some time away from the stimulating atmosphere of the university to see if I could "settle down". A helpful GP furnished me with a medical certificate and an interview with Dr Berndt of the Anthropology Department gave me the support I needed to defer my final exams until January. Friends in the wheat-belt agreed to accept me as a long term working guest on their extensive farm. I spend a month as a farm worker and guest, reading theology in the evenings and working in the paddocks by day.

My prescription proved effective. Returning to study in December, I found that I was able to lead the kind of quiet existence needed to complete my assignments and prepare myself for the exams. In the event, I passed both units with a credit, so all was well. I remember how carefully I learned to monitor the level of my stimulus and engagement with others. I noted how easily my anxiety arose to disturbing levels if I did not maintain a fairly even kind of life. The doctor had prescribed a mild tranquilliser to deal with these occasional bursts of anxiety.

By this stage of my education, the language of depression and anxiety had become quite familiar to me, but the notion of a manic episode was not something I considered at all. This second episode — while very different from the first — strengthened in me the awareness that my emotional stability was not something I could take for granted, and that certain kinds of stress were best avoided. I was widely considered to be the next in line to lead the University Evangelical Union, and to the surprise of many I declined the position and put forward a younger friend to take on the role. After the episode in my final year, I knew I could not be at all sure that taking such a prominent role would not render me immobile again.

With my graduation from university, it was time to take up my chosen career in high school teaching. Naturally, this presented plenty of challenges to the sheltered and serious young man I was. Dealing with unruly students who had none of my own interest in learning proved exasperating and exhausting, and I was dissuaded from an early resignation by an older Christian friend who had preceded me along this way. He had also experienced emotional exhaustion and depression, and was deeply sensitive to the emotional side of the difficulties I experienced in my first years of teaching. At his advice, I took the opportunity of a visit to Melbourne to consult with a psychiatrist — such specialists were unknown in Perth at this time!

During this consultation, I was advised that there was no major issue in my psychological health but that I would probably need to deal with recurring episodes of anxiety. It was recommended that I make use of one of the mild tranquillisers that were now on the market, such medications as Librium or Valium, member of the benzodiazepine family. There was reassurance in this diagnosis, although perhaps a bit of a shock to think that I might need to use medication to treat my condition.

Another aspect of my anxiety symptoms occupied my reflection. Having struggled with masturbation as a young man, and finding no outlet for sexual expression in my lifestyle, it began to occur to me that my strong sexual interests might be a cause of some of my distress. I was not disturbed at all by the insistence of my sexual interest, and was strongly attracted to the young women of my acquaintance, but premarital sexual activity was socially proscribed in these days, especially in my religious sub-culture. My concern was to find a good way to find satisfaction in this area of my life — and this inevitably meant marriage!

After a few, quite happy but ultimately unsuccessful, romantic attachments, I met the woman with whom I would spend my next thirty-five years. After a whirl-wind romance, Peta and I were married in 1967 and my life took a new turn. By this stage, I had managed to consolidate my career in teaching and to make a beginning in theological education. I felt confident that marriage would spell the end of any emotional disturbance in my life and that henceforth my career and private life would proceed smoothly. However, in the months following our wedding, I discovered how mistaken I was.

Instead of a life of bliss, I continued much the same as before, and during this period entered into a severely debilitating depression. Looking back, I can list several factors behind my distress. First, I guess would be disappointment, not disappointment with my partner or the good elements of our marriage, but disappointment that my unrealistic hopes for a "new me" had not materialised. In addition, marriage involved a radical change of home arrangements, as I moved out of my parents' home and set up a new household with my wife. Comfort and familiarity were replaced with a rather Spartan existence and, obviously, new relationships. In particular, I found it very difficult to feel comfortable as a member of my wife's rather noisy extended family.

Of course, there was the ongoing challenge of my professional duties as a high school teacher to unruly students, and, in addition, I had agreed to lead a Beach Mission team and conduct a childrens special service mission in a sea-side town over the summer. The range of these challenges somehow proved beyond me, and I desperately sought to withdraw to a safe place. None was available and I took long solitary walks in the evening, seeking to calm my troubled spirit.

About this episode I did use the word depression, but I told no one except my young wife what was going on with me. She had never encountered such a thing yet took it all in good spirit. So severe were my feelings of dejection that I sought medical assistance. The GP correctly diagnosed depression and recommended a course of tricyclic antidepressants, which were just then coming onto the market. I was reluctant to go down this track and sceptical that such a course would assist, but agreed to go along with it.

Within a couple of weeks — as if by magic — my mood lifted and I found I was able to handle the negative emotions and get on with my work and my leadership role. With the help of the medications, my own determination to succeed and the support of my wife, I completed all assignments and then took a good holiday in the remainder of the summer break.[5] The following year, we moved to Kalgoorlie, and here enjoyed a real first year of married life without any undesired incidents. Life was picking up for us and we looked forward to a long marriage and further adventures together.

THE DEVELOPMENT OF INSIGHT

Any memoir is of a piece with its setting in time and place and mine is no exception. Growing up in the 1950s in Australia I was part of a "lucky" generation, as we experienced economic prosperity and political stability. But this was also a time when the parenting approach of most adults was one of "benign neglect" — "adolescence" had not yet been invented or discovered, whatever is the right word. I entered adolescence in a home which knew nothing of its strain and difficulties. My parents were very caring individuals, but they were in many ways unprepared for the modern world which I was entering. They saw their responsibility more in terms of providing physical and emotional stability than of monitoring the psychological ups and downs of their children's lives.[6]

Having lived through the Great Depression, they had learnt the art of survival. Married while Dad was serving in the Australian Air Force, they had their first son while the Second World War still raged on our doorstep. My earliest days were spent in very close connection with my mother while Dad was away doing military service. His return in 1945 created something of a crisis in my secure world. In time, I came to accept and draw close to him, but it took a while for me to accept his gentle and loving presence. In the 1950s, we began to enjoy the fruits of peace and post-war prosperity, but in many ways, we were living in a dark age, especially in the understanding and treatment of mental illness.

Survivors of the Depression and War allowed no space for weakness or self-indulgence, and as a boy I was instilled with this ethos and the need to be self-sufficient. We knew of mental cases, but during this time the only treatment options were isolation in an asylum or shock therapy. To admit to a psychological problem was to envisage that you might end up with one of these outcomes. Although the 50s saw great progress in the development of anti-depressive medications, these results and their therapeutic benefits took some time to filter down to the average person in the street.

I benefitted from advances in the understanding and treatment of mental illness occurring in the 1950s. While I was acquainted with the class of mild tranquilliser — the benzodiazepines — from an early stage, it was the prescription of the newer antidepressant medication, amitriptyline, which brought about the remarkable lifting of my mood in 1967. This breakthrough enabled me to complete my tasks for the year and approach my future with confidence.

The impact of this intervention was quite profound. Having been told earlier in my journey that I might need to have recourse throughout my life to the use of mild tranquillisers, I was already coming into the world of psychotropic medications. Of course, no one likes to be told they may need to use a medication throughout their life, and I saw the use of tranquillisers as a less than desirable treatment method. However, it was with the recourse to antidepressant medication that the big step was made for me.

By now, I had learned that depression could recur and that it could be crippling of initiative and satisfaction in life. Yet I also had discovered that treatment was possible with prescribed medication; the devastating effects of depression were not beyond amelioration. The strength and persistence of the depressive symptoms and their ability to render me miserable and dysfunctional made the exploration of this medication necessary. By the time of this second depressive experience, it was clear that I suffered from an episodic depressive condition and the successful treatment of this depression with an early tricyclic medication seemed nothing short of miraculous. Neither of these discoveries filled me with great joy, but there was some relief in the sense that there was indeed a way forward for me. Would religion feature in this forward pathway?

What impact did an emerging theological awareness have when coupled with growing psychological insight? Looking back at the memoir outlined above, it would be very easy to draw the inference that a troubled adolescent found solace in the security of a strict religious society and that his religion was a useful tool — perhaps some kind of crutch — that enabled him to negotiate the difficult transitions of the teenage years. With such a viewpoint, it might then be expected that with greater psychological insight and a supportive environment it would be only a matter of time before the religious tool outlived its usefulness and adulthood would bring a falling away of this orientation.

However, I did not choose to take this well-worn interpretive pathway. With growing theological understanding, I saw that while psychological readings of personal history have some interpretive value, they did not really address issues of the validity of religious experience or indeed the truth of theological claims. Unless, that is, one vested them with a kind of ultimacy: my theological training had alerted me to the dangers of misplacing a sense of the ultimate on issues or interpretations other than God. Further, I was energised to think in new ways about the religious dimension, to pose new concepts of God and different understandings of the human relationship with God.

Insight into my own condition emerged only gradually. While my memoir begins with a severe depressive episode, the most common distress I experienced was anxiety. I was anxious at school, I suffered a rather acute social phobia as I tried to find my way into the boys' group and experienced other anxieties while at university. Before the advent of the antidepressants on the market, the only common psychotropic medication was the minor tranquilliser. Early on, I encountered Librium and later Valium, both members of the Benzodiazepine family of drugs. Although they later fell into disfavour, these early medications were very effective in treating anxiety disorders. A psychiatric consultation I had during the 70s — before my first real engagement in psychiatric treatment — suggested to me that I would probably need to use these medications occasionally throughout my life.

I realised that these symptoms need not have the final say in my life, and that medical science offered me a way out. Although I did not like the idea of using such medication on an ongoing basis, I developed a new confidence. I was able to see that this depression condition need not spell the end of my aspirations and hopes for future life. The third depressive episode, during my studies in Melbourne, confirmed this self-diagnosis, and it was on this occasion that I was in a position to seek ongoing psychiatric consultation. At that time, as I have said, it was common to treat depression and anxiety as closely related conditions and to use appropriate medications for each. To this third incident we now turn.

3: CRISIS

Following a satisfying year in Kalgoorlie, we moved to Melbourne so that I could complete academic studies in theology. An exciting new phase of life was opening up for us and we both revelled in the cultural diversity and intellectual stimulation of Melbourne in the late sixties. However, it was here that my next episode of depression struck. This time, I had a language and some new strategies to deal with the condition.

On this occasion, there was a theological component to the distress I experienced. The intimate conservative theological cocoon of my adolescence was being broken asunder by the currents of contemporary theology encountered in Melbourne. I found myself drawn to the ethical sensitivity on social issues of the "liberals" rather than the more narrow, individualistic views of the "evangelicals". Yet neither of these positions seemed to me to be essentially linked to a theological stance. I did not see the need wholly to abandon the theological convictions of my youth. I was a thinker in transition, and yet I found these considerations occasioned a certain amount of anxiety. Could all the people who had nurtured me be in the wrong, and did I need to turn my back on them? Perhaps it was as much an issue of loyalty as it was actual theology that occasioned the distress.

I sought to share with some of my conservative friends the challenges I was facing, and found that they had no sympathy at all. I remember a trip to Sydney when I met with a group of old mates, only to find myself excluded from the intimacy of the bonds I had experienced and to feel that they were talking about me, rather than to me. Following upon this trip, the anxiety began to grow more intense. I felt "outside" the circle that had nurtured me, even though I was grappling with significant theological issues in an open-minded and constructive manner.

There was a summer during which I engaged in the intriguing intellectual puzzle of deciding whether I was still an "evangelical" or had become a "liberal" as my friends averred. This irresolution, coupled with the cold rejection of my closer friends, pitched me into a position of anxious isolation. I found I could not "solve" the dilemma I faced — in retrospect it was a false problem — and the only result was that I began the New Year once again feeling severely anxious and alone. Depression soon followed. I felt that I had dug myself into a hole and that it was all of my own doing. Fortunately, this time help was available.

During this my second year of theological study, we were required to have a "small group" experience. With trained facilitators, we were encouraged to "open up" to one another, or as the colourful phrase of the day went, to "spill our guts", and to reflect together on our processes of personal and professional formation. This was a new departure for theological education in Australia, and we did not realise we were in the vanguard of a whole new approach to ministerial training. In the course of my small group work, I could not hide the state of my own psyche, and the depth of my depression and the associated anxiety soon became apparent to my sensitive group leader. As he was himself undergoing psycho-therapy with one of the leading psychiatrists of Melbourne, he recommended that I get myself into therapy. In 1970, this was a radical proposal as we were sure that only crazy and insecure people needed that kind of intervention. My depression was crippling enough, however, that I decided to follow Peter's suggestion and soon found myself the patient of a psychiatrist.

I was immediately prescribed a combination of tricyclic antidepressants and a mild tranquilliser. The drug therapy worked wonders on my mood and my capacity to enjoy life and engage fully with my studies. For the first time, I discovered I had an insightful and powerful ally in my struggle to find my own way of life. The psychiatrist introduced me to theories of identity formation and placed my current depression in the context of an ongoing struggle to identify and claim my own person. Under this attention, I truly thrived, making substantial headway in my theological understanding and having the confidence at the end of this period to travel overseas with the purpose of undertaking higher academic studies.

With good treatment and growing insight into the roots of my discomfort, I came to embrace the critical theology I was learning and to discern that there were ways within it to adhere to some of my earliest theological convictions. I could indeed forge my own theological path, without falling into the usual camps and groupings. I was learning that theological reflection requires knowledge, insight and subtlety in modes of thought and analysis. I was also learning that the judicious use of medication could establish long patterns of emotional stability and intellectual productivity. Not all would agree, however, on what constituted a "judicious" use, as I was soon to discover in another place.

FACING THE FUTURE

The early experiences recounted in this chapter set me up to face my future with hope. I had gained considerable self-knowledge concerning my own vulnerabilities and my tendency to react to sustained stress with depression. I was acutely aware of the kinds of situation that might cause such stress, especially those that related to my living conditions and my identity as a practising Christian. Early in our married life, we were offered the opportunity to become a kind of house parents to a group of adolescent folk with some religious orientation. While the idea of the job and the conditions of the employment appealed to me, I immediately knew that the stress involved in fulfilling such a position would not be good for me. I dismissed the possibility of taking up this work.

On the other hand, I was eager to challenge myself to grow intellectually. I had dreamed of being an academic theologian, of teaching and writing within my chosen field. The years of preparation had been full of uncertainty. My academic beginnings in Perth and Melbourne had shown moments of promise and also long periods when my direction seemed clouded. Continually throughout this period, however, the dream remained alive and I pursued it with some vigour, aided and encouraged by my young wife. She was ambitious for me, as I was ambitious for myself. Receiving only a second class honours degree in 1970 after an indifferent performance on a difficult Hebrew language paper, I felt that perhaps my ambitions were too grand, but still a better option did not present itself. I determined to seek graduate studies in theology in 1971.

It was the British mail strike of that year that caused me to go to the USA for graduate studies, rather than my preferred United Kingdom. I applied in January for a study position at King's College, London, early in the year, and did not hear any response to my application. Fearing that the reply might be in the negative, I devised a back-up plan for study in the United States, namely at Princeton Theological Seminary or Yale Divinity School. In the days before email, mobile phones or texts, the mail strike covered all forms of communication including telecommunication out of the United Kingdom, and did not end until early April. Imagine my surprise in mid-April to receive acceptances from all three of my applications, including a WCC Scholarship to study at Princeton!

The draw-card to study at London was Professor Peter Ackroyd, with whom I had worked briefly at Melbourne. Professor Ackroyd had indicated to me that life in the United Kingdom was difficult for theological students at this time, and sources of funding might be difficult to find. In the meantime, I had learnt about the study opportunities at Yale and had gained some familiarity with the work of Dr Brevard Childs. In Melbourne, I had read with great interest his *Myth and Reality in the Old Testament*. On reflection, it seemed that the life of a theological student might be more fully supported in the United States. At that time, too, I was beginning to feel that theological education needed to embrace some of the newer models that were coming out of the USA. It seemed that graduate study in that country might better fit me for future work within the Australian setting.

Although I had always dreamed of travelling to the UK, the balance of factors led to a major shift in my thinking and we resolved to travel to the USA to take up studies at Yale Divinity School. I felt the scholars working there were superior to those at Princeton Seminary, so resolved to turn down the scholarship that was on offer. The decision was a fusion of idealism and practicality, not giving all the weight to either side of the equation. So, it was in August 1971, we found ourselves inhabiting a rather small but comfortable on-campus apartment at Yale Divinity School.

In the event, I chose a demanding course of study at one of the best universities in the world. In 1971, I enrolled in a Master's program at Yale University Divinity School. Naturally enough, the challenges of a new place and new study opportunities left me at times with fairly serious anxiety symptoms, so I resolved that it might be best to seek early medication rather than suffer a full-blown depressive episode. When I sought through the Student Health scheme to renew the medications I was on in Australia, I ran into a buzz saw. Suddenly the medical staff raised the alarm. A student seeking a prescription of psychotropic medications! No doubt they had seen the abuse of some of these medications among their young patients and were concerned that I was heading down a wrong path. I was speedily referred to a counsellor, who did not have the authority to prescribe medication. So, the Student Health Scheme provided counselling but not treatment by medication for students.

If it had seemed that in coming to the USA I was moving away from the rather pre-modern approaches to psychological care that were standard in Australia at that time, I was to learn that there were other agendas running and what I had hoped in terms of a smooth transition would be anything but. While I found ways of dealing with these issues, my wife now experienced for the first time a major depressive episode. The shoe was on the other foot! With the help of a Pastoral Counsellor, she came to an understanding of her feelings and we moved into our life in the USA with high expectations of a future in academic study and teaching. I had understood that my depressions were likely to recur throughout my life, and that support and counselling could be found that enabled me to face this as a challenge which could certainly be surmounted.

With the move to the United States of America we had come into a culture that was already saturated with therapeutic insights. Perth of the 1950s seemed far away! Although my immediate transition into this environment was somewhat bumpy, we soon came to feel at home here and were encouraged in many ways to explore more fully the roots and consequences of our psychological disturbances. We also encountered a much more sophisticated level of theological scholarship and debate, and it became a setting in which we truly thrived.

During all this period, I was being trained as a theologian, and my understanding of my own psychological vulnerabilities did not pose a major issue with what I was coming to understand of this discipline. Stimulating as these studies were in an intellectual sense, they also posed new possibilities for the religious life and the life of prayer. When, for example, I brought an issue of personal stress to the spiritual teacher, Dr Henri Nouwen, he suggested a week with the Trappists as a suitable therapy for me. Now I was introduced to prayer that is of a more contemplative nature, one that involves music and silence rather that words and lists. While I had never been a "natural" when it comes to prayer, I began to explore new ways of seeking to express my relationship with God in Christ. Again, I was fortunate that people I met, like Henri Nouwen and the psychiatrist I consulted in Melbourne, were people of the highest calibre who were not inclined to offer reductive accounts of religious experience, nor, heaven forbid, doctrinaire Freudianism, who might have wanted me to rid myself of the illusions of religion.

I have already alluded to the possibility that prayer might be significant in relation to depression, and have so far advanced the view that, for the person suffering from depression, prayer seems like a desperate "last resort". Now I was beginning to see prayer in a new light. This had broader consequences as we shall see in the next section.

A CLOSER LOOK AT PRAYER

During a depressive episode, it was very difficult for me to enter into or to develop relationships with others.[7] I became isolated in my own mood and sadness. With the loss of meaning and purpose and the emergence of a kind of malaise, it seemed overly difficult to relate to people outside the mood. Yet when the depression lifted, normality returned and relationships could be developed. It now appeared that what was true of human relationships was also true of my relationship with God and with my own spirit. The separation I experienced cut right to the quick that separates one person from another, and even a person from themself. [8]

These episodic dips into depression also seemed to deprive me of any sense of a relationship with God. They were not only dark times of sadness, they were for me also god-less periods. Prayer, which seems a normal part of human life, at these times became beyond reach. It seemed in the darkness that indeed there was no God and prayer was simply an illusory way of talking to one-self. I was discovering in practice what was well known in care of depressed persons, that the carer needed to pray *for* them because they were incapable of praying for themselves. I found my mind turning to the question of what exactly is prayer, especially as reflected in the book of prayers known as the Psalms. My thought proceeded in the following way.

For most people, prayer signifies a cry for help in a desperate situation. The Psalmist writes:

> Out of the depths I cry to you, O Lord,
>
> Lord, hear my voice!
>
> Let your ears be attentive
>
> to the voice of my supplications! (Psalm 130)

The psalmist speaks out of an earlier, in some ways "simpler" age. Today, most maladies have an appropriate cure, so that it has become common to see this kind of cry as the voice of superstition or immaturity. For many, it is a cry of "last resort"; even the atheists in the trenches admit to such a plea. Yet our enlightened age does not really believe in the value of such a prayer. Of course, the more we learn the more we realise how little we know, and to some observers our modern confidence in rational and medical solutions to every problem is beginning to appear as a case of optimistic over-reach. In the vast history of human culture, the range of settings in which a human person has sought for aid is very wide, and will probably continue well into the future. It seems to be part and parcel of our very humanity to seek for a higher order of aid in difficult times, and who can really say that such a cry is without real effect?

My beginnings in prayer had much to do with "prayer lists", compendiums of good causes and needy individuals for whom I undertook to plead their case with the divine. It took some time for me to realise how narrow is this concept of prayer, as if God were some kind of heavenly Father Christmas who was there to attend to the request of human supplicants. Prayer as the cry to distress is not invalid, and this reflex may be evidence of a gut-level belief in God, but as a person's main mode of prayer it suffers from a severely truncated view of God. As Bob Dylan parodies in the wonderful line from his song "Slow Train Comin'":

> You think he's just an errand boy
>
> to satisfy your wandering desires.

Of course, we should not expect a fully developed view of God from the proverbial atheists in the trenches! But if we read further in the Psalms, we find that this type of cry in *extremis* is a small part of the prayer experience. A large part of prayer, as I have suggested above, is more in the mode of waiting.

> I wait for the Lord, my soul waits,
>
> and in his word I hope;
>
> my soul waits for the Lord,
>
> more than those who watch for the morning,
>
> more than those who watch for the morning. (Psalm 130)

Then, beside the prayer of desperation, and the prayer of waiting, is the cry of joy or exultation.

> Make a joyful noise to God, all the earth,
>
> sing the glory of his name;
>
> give to him glorious praise. (Psalm 66)

From desperate need to the joy that struggles to find words, all these states of mind are rendered in prayer to God. The Psalms make a wonderful lesson book for prayer, to one raised in our strangely a-theistic age.

Of course, there is place too for shame and lament. All of us sense our own inadequacies, and at times a sense of personal failure is acute. The Psalmist knew this aspect, and knew too what to do with it. Personal failure — especially of a moral nature — called for confession before the God who stood for ultimate righteousness and also mercy.

Have mercy on me, O God,
according to your unfailing love…
Wash away all my iniquity
and cleanse me from my sin.

Against you, you only, have I sinned
and done what is evil in your sight. (Psalm 51, NIV)

For the person with a sense of the divine, informed by the Judeo-Christian heritage, God is more than a cosmic judge; above all, God is the source of redeeming love. So, the recourse to the mercy of God for both forgiveness and cleansing is naturally available. While God can function as the judge and exemplar of moral perfection, in this relationship God is also the font of mercy and new beginnings.

Yet this is precisely what disappears during a depressive episode. God, it seems, joins the general chorus of criticism and condemnation. And theological therapy seems quite useless at this point. What has become clear to me is that religious faith itself needs to undergo a modulation for the person suffering with depression. Rather than a belief in God's love and a sense of God's caring presence, faith might be better understood as a kind of hope or trust, hope or trust that this too will pass, and that the sense of easy access to the divine presence is something we live to hope for. By no means always present, the sense of the redeeming activity of God in one's life, is a gift of grace, one that sometimes cannot be grasped. This view of faith corresponds with a somewhat different understanding of prayer — prayer as a kind of waiting upon the divine presence. Sometimes waiting in silence, always waiting in hope. Sometimes, hope beyond hope. Even when the experience — the effects, the confidence — of prayer is lacking, it is still possible to exercise the will and affirm that there is something, Someone, beyond our own experience. Hope in that possibility is then an exercise of faith.

4: CONSOLIDATION

The Yale years were marked by some dramatic ups and downs: the birth of our first child Creina certainly marking a high point, the severe depression of my wife marking a real low. In 1973, I was fortunate to gain a three-year doctoral fellowship to complete a Ph.D. at Emory University, in the field of Systematic Theology. These years of graduate study were a very rich time for us as a couple, as we involved ourselves in the life of a renewing neighbourhood in inner Atlanta, and considerably enriched our rather poverty-stricken experience of the life of the sixties and seventies. A serious and upright couple, we allowed our hair to hang down as was the fashion of the day, and experienced a range of enriching friendships and experiences beyond the pale of the Church. In the free-swinging life of a graduate student, there was ample room for the kinds of mood swings I had come to expect as my normal lot in life. My wife had no recurrence of the depression she had experienced in New Haven, and our lives seemed rich beyond measure.

During this period of relative freedom, I was able to ride the ups and downs of my moods in a free-wheeling way. With no daily pressures, I could take time to accommodate my lows by lying low, and my highs by living it up! During this time, I sought the counsel of a pastoral counsellor, who assisted me to understand the foundations of my depression in my relationship with my father. I developed a close relationship with this man, which in some ways enabled me to work out many of the things I had missed in my relationship with my own father.

CLINICAL DIAGNOSIS

In April 1978, I was appointed Assistant Professor of Theology at United Theological Seminary in Dayton, Ohio. Dayton was no Atlanta. In the late 70s, it was a city down on its heels, as heavy industry fled the old Industrial East and relocated to the South and West. Overnight, we had become a respectable professional family and I knuckled down to master the profession of academic teaching. One thing was immediately clear. I could not afford the kind of free-wheeling life style of the Atlanta years. I needed regular sleep and regular waking hours to support the life of discipline and work that faced me. Early, I went to see my GP about problems sleeping, and he, examining my irises, commented that my nervous impulses were working overtime. I believe it was with help in sleeping in mind that he prescribed me a mild antidepressant of the tricyclic form. Fairly soon, I found myself in the rooms of a consulting psychiatrist rehearsing again the history of my struggles.

This psychiatrist concluded that I would need to accustom myself to ongoing treatment for depression and anxiety with the use of antidepressants and some form of occasional anxiety medication. He dismissed as romantic my notion that I might somehow manage to break free of this pattern and find personal wholeness by personal adjustment without the aid of medication. To his mind, the pattern of regular episodic depression had established itself and my best and only course was to accept this and work within the parametres of the treatment plan he outlined. So began a long period of relative stability, during which I established my career and published my articles and books. I was rewarded with promotion through the ranks of Associate Professor to full Professor of Theology in 1987. My position was then tenured, and I coined the phrase, "Now I am tenured and terminal". It was never my intention to spend the rest of my life in the United States of America!

In many ways, the years in Dayton formed the fulfilment of all I had worked and hoped for in the preceding years. I enjoyed my work and was grateful for all the rewards my position accorded me. Yet somehow I did not feel it was my destiny to remain as a tenured Professor of Theology in the Mid-West of the United States. A visit home to Australia in 1983 had briefly reunited me with the landscape I had grown up with. So strong was the effect of these sights that I resolved to spend an upcoming Sabbatical in Perth researching images of the landscape in Australian literature. Out of this research, my first book was written and published in 1989, *A Sense of Place: A Christian Theology of the Land*. The book secured my tenure but in a way cemented my determination to return to Australia. I began seeking an academic position in Australia. Although I gained several interviews, no contract was ever offered, so in 1988 I resolved on one last attempt to gain a position, in Adelaide, failing which I would seek a parish appointment in Australia. Again I was interviewed, but the position went to another; instead, in January 1989, I found myself appointed as Minister of the Word at the Floreat Parish of the Uniting Church in a western suburb of Perth, my old home town and my old home congregation!

This dramatic turn signalled something of a spiritual rebirth for me as a person and as a professional. The years in the USA had been marked by regular involvement in the life of the local Church and teaching theology at the Seminary, but it had not called forth from me new ventures in faith and discipleship. There was any easy marriage between my Christian faith and the life-styles we adopted in Atlanta and Dayton. It seemed that God was in his heaven and all was well in the world. I was not called upon to reveal my own spiritual self to any great extent. But now as a parish minister, I was suddenly the key exemplar of Christian living and thinking for a whole community of people. Feeling ready for this, I threw myself into the life of the congregation, and found a whole new vocation for myself.

INSIGHT DEEPENS

I look back now on the twenty years I spent as Professor of Theology and then as a Parish Minister at Floreat as being my most stable years. I worked hard at both jobs and in different ways did well at both of them. In the next phase of my life, all this was lost, so in considering this period it's perhaps worth asking what made for its stability, and how my mental state reflected what was happening in the broader spheres of my life.

First must count the fact that we were in a stable relationship. While there had been some ups and downs in the Atlanta year, Dayton and Floreat found us a steady married couple, taken up with professional work and raising a family. Second, our employment was steady and the income stream sufficient for our needs and the needs of our growing family. The major stressors of financial or relational hardship were not factors in this period. From my personal point of view must count the fact that in addition to these contextual factors, I was working out of a firm diagnosis and received steady and consistent psychiatric support and guidance. It was clear I had a recurrent pattern of depression which required ongoing medical treatment. So long as I was happy to accept this diagnosis and follow the treatment plans prescribed, there was no need for change or disruption. Of course, from time to time I rebelled against this, and tried "going off the medication". My wife was always opposed to this experiment, and the first to call me back to the old diagnosis and treatment when she noticed irritability and unhappiness creeping into our lives!

A fourth factor is worth mentioning, which came into action in the Ministry phase of this narrative. With our return to Australia in 1989, I decided I could no longer delay my lifetime ambitions in relation to farming. Within six months of our return, I began hunting down small properties on the outskirts of Perth for possible purchase. Our searches led us to the beautiful Chittering valley one hour north of Perth where at the close of that year we were able to purchase a hill-side property of some 55 acres. With what untold joy did I purchase this property in fulfilment of a dream I had first conceived over thirty years previously, after a visit with my uncle in Albany.

It might be thought — following on my earlier recollections — that it was difficult to persuade my father to take an interest in the farm. The opposite was the case! He couldn't wait to join me in visiting and constructing first dreams, then sheds, fences and pathways on this property! During the years of my ministry, Dad and I had a fixed appointment to travel to and work on the farm on my free Mondays. So faithful was this now old man that I looked at him struggling one day with a gate and a voice inside said, "Whatever was once wrong, Dad, is all forgiven". By this stage of my life, I knew that there was much to forgive. The man whose emotional absence when his teenaged son most needed him was now fully present in ways I could not have imagined. All is forgiven, I softly intoned. I will never complain again about anything you do or say. A deep bond of shared labour and aspiration formed between us in those last years of his life. I wouldn't have missed it for anything, and this was perhaps the real reason for my return to Australia and forsaking the academic career I had fashioned in the USA.

If depression is the absence of joy, it is worth noting this first sign of a return of joy into my life. It had the power to dispel the darkness and to shed love where once there had been mistrust and fear. Following a busy week in the parish, it became my practice to retire to the farm on Sunday evening and Monday and to enter a space of quietness, or physical work in companionship often with my father, and of prayer. The week of work provided plenty of jumping off points for my reflection on the reality of God in my life and the lives of my parishioners. This time — often quiet hours of solitude — deepened my somewhat fitful life of prayer into something that I anticipated eagerly and entered into gladly. Joy was at work not only in my access to this place, but also in my sense that here was a place where God was present and could be waited upon. During this stage too, the realisation grew that God was not a separate person, outside and beyond myself, but in fact the very life within which I and my parishioners lived and moved. The mystery of God deepened. Not only was God too far beyond my mind to comprehend: God was too deeply within us to be grasped.[9]

It was during this period that I began to become more serious about my writing, especially of poetry. One of the poems of the 1980s speaks directly of the experience of depression.

It comes like the dew overnight.
Next morning it's there,
everything is covered.

Phases of the moon move blood.
Ocean tides creep into
hidden estuaries,
familiar marshlands.
Gently, mysteriously,
seepage enters me.

I wake to fear
some sudden
unbidden
descent.

I believe that in writing about the darker aspects of one's experience, those experiences are opened up to the light of day, and in that process some of the pain and fear they may generate are dissipated. Giving a name to a condition was in an earlier phase of my life a tremendous aid to understanding and management. Developing images and lines of reflection, which poetry enables, is an important part of the therapeutic process. Finding this kind of expression gives one a handle on experience and makes the necessary adjustments of real life more manageable.

So passed the bulk of my professional life. I succeeded as an academic theologian and I succeeded as a professional Minister of the Uniting Church. But to what extent was I running on inherited capital? Certainly, my learnings for ten years as a professor of theology and years in graduate school had filled my head with ideas and perspectives relevant for my ministry. I was full of a sense of confidence and awareness of the theological dimensions of my work. But what about the personal, the spiritual? Was my new vocation sustainable? By the end of 1995, after six years in the ministry, I was finding myself drained and depleted. It was at this time that I embarked on the Retreat I detail in the Epilogue to these chapters.

5: INTERRUPTION

NEW CHALLENGE

During this long period of professional consolidation, there were certainly times of emotional challenge. As my period in the parish seemed to be reaching an end, I searched in vain for academic positions throughout Australia. Although I had been a regular sessional Lecturer in the Perth Theological Hall, my attempts to move into a full-time position were stymied. The most interesting instance was the last time I applied for the position of Lecturer in Theology in Perth in 1997. The interview process occurred during a very hot month of February, and we had just moved into a rather poorly cooled little asbestos house. I so much wanted to be successful in this application but found myself quite unable to prepare for the presentations I was to give. Whether it was the heat or my level of anxiety about the prospect, I completely blew the interview process, somehow managing to get myself spooked by the formal process. In one ill-judged performance, I managed to completely throw away any chance I had for appointment.

In retrospect, it seemed to me that I had no effective way of managing the anxiety of the situation or of convincing myself to do my best work for this interview process. Because of my long association with the Perth Theological Hall and my position as a respected Minister and teacher within the Synod, I had been widely expected to win the position. The failure to do was so professionally devastating and publicly humiliating. I did not know how to interpret it other than a clear indication that my academic ambitions were misguided and that I should henceforth focus my energies in other directions. I was ambitious but not so single-mindedly so that I could only redouble my efforts until I succeeded. I beat a strategic retreat from a long-held ambition and sense of vocation.

A new possibility presented itself when the National Assembly of the Uniting Church resolved to establish a new agency to deal with issues of theology and discipleship. This position seemed to offer some scope for someone with academic training in theology to serve directly the wider church's need for theologically based leadership. Still, I was reluctant to launch myself into an unknown role on a national stage with which I was unfamiliar. With my wife, I took a weekend holiday on Rottnest Island to make my decision. Reading the biography of Alan Walker, I came quite suddenly to the view that I could manage national leadership, my mood suddenly shifted from one of mild depression to something approaching elation. A new wave of self-confidence engulfed me, and I decided to offer myself for the position. I had been encouraged both by the national president of the Church and my wife, and thus I was appointed and began one of the most disastrous phases of my life and career!

MANIC EPISODE

I found the new position stimulating and challenging. I travelled between five capital cities in Australia to supervise the running of four national working groups — in theology, worship, mission and evangelism. I was required to be a public face of the Church, appearing at meetings and making radio broadcasts. I loved the early days of the job and revelled in my new-found voice. But underneath, trouble was brewing. My wife suffered a rather severe depression, was unable to find suitable work, and hated the house we had been assigned. This was all bad enough, but with my public exposure and constant travel, things did not go well in our relationship. A recurrence of back trouble—due to sleeping in many strange and below standard beds, not to mention frequent air travel—laid me low for the period of the Sydney Olympics in 2000.

What was the spiritual impact of these events? I no longer had the farm to retire to for periods of silence and prayer. In a new city, belonging to a new congregation, and most often on the road, I cannot recall times when I drew back to the silence and wonder of the presence of God. While work was demanding, I seemed to have the skills needed to tackle the work, and none of it required the deep presence with others in spirit that pastoral ministry required of me. Prayer became largely a public exercise, and I did not notice that it had largely dropped out of my private experience.

Matters deteriorated so much in our marriage that we entered a trial separation during the year 2000. During this period, I was required to lead a National Consultation on Theology. The stressors were indeed piling up. I had been confirmed in my diagnosis and treatment for Major Episodic Depression but this left me quite unprepared for what eventuated, so much so, that like my very first episode, I failed to recognise it until it had already cost me my job and possibly my marriage. Things reached a head during the National Consultation and the Assembly meeting which followed. Although I had prepared well for this with very disciplined labour over many months, the increased stress of the event and the need to perform publicly precipitated me into my first and only "manic" episode.

I found myself rejoicing in boundless energy for meeting people and felt assured in my personal charm and wit. I awoke each morning eager to get out of bed and take a morning walk with my dog through the neighbouring golf course. The confidence that had propelled me into this prominent position seemed to be carrying me along to make a great showing of the performance of my duties. Little did I realise I was actually making a clown of myself and that my colleagues were not impressed. Without knowing in the least what was going on, I was actually exhibiting all the signs of mania. It was by no means "hyper-mania" and I did not do anything truly outrageous or spend vast sums of money. But such was the attention to my public performance, such were the expectations of one in my position, that my loss of my usual modesty and the misalignment of my judgments were painfully apparent to others. My boss could tell that there was something "off" in the way I was presenting myself publicly and ordered me to take a few quite weeks of leave. I was being treated at the time for depression and taking anti-depressants. When my supervisor suggested that perhaps I was not well, I asked for a reference from my treating psychiatrist and his note assured my boss that I was mentally well. A possible explanation and exoneration were thereby ruled out.

The trouble was that I wasn't at all well; and the worst of it was that I had no idea. Given the endorsement of my mental health from my psychiatrist, the national Church urged me to resign on health grounds. My refusal to do so was, I believe, one of the manic symptoms of my illness. It was a mess and could not end well. I was 57, and with my marriage on the rocks and my career finished, I felt that my life had suddenly fallen to pieces. Yet removal of the stress of the performance of high profile public duties and a time of quietness to reflect, enabled me to recover quite rapidly. I found work as a humble parish minister. Given a short congregational assignment, I poured my heart into this work and quietly "worked out my own salvation".

It took some months, however, for me to realise the psychological implications of what had happened. My firm diagnosis and treatment for Major Episodic Depression served to mask the real situation here, and the letter of my treating psychiatrist only deepened the career implications of this episode. By this time, however, new developments in the understanding and treatment of depression had led to a new focus on "bipolar disorders". It was well known that most anxiety and depressive follow somewhat cyclical patterns, with highs and lows alternating. When I sought the help of another prominent psychiatrist, I was promptly diagnosed as mild manic depressive. So began a new phase of my treatment and understanding of my journey.

One after another of the old and new "mood stabilisers", from lithium to olanzapine and fluoxetine were prescribed and trialled. While this matter was pursued with great conviction on the part of my therapist, the results for me were anything but encouraging. I experienced no stabilising effect, and meanwhile my depression seemed to deepen. The psychiatrist now made a sudden switch to an older tricyclic medication, massively increasing the dosage until my hands shook and I felt like I was being poisoned. In fact, I was, and at my own insistence, the dosages of medication were reduced until I began to feel like myself again.

It took some time for sanity to prevail. Treatment for bipolar was not helping my function, and a sudden switch to massive doses of tricyclics only gave me toxic symptoms. The old regime had worked successfully for decades and the only reason not to let it resume was the intoxication of a new diagnosis. Enticing as a new medical diagnosis was, my case clearly didn't fit into the text-book definition. The new psychiatrist was too moved, it seems, by theory to engage fully with the particularity of my individual symptoms. Although my regular psychiatrist had failed to discern a manic episode for what it was, his patient observation over many years had produced sound insight into the best treatment of my condition.

These insights were often hard won, and exacted a price not only in terms of personal comfort but also in relation to work performance and advancement. It is perhaps something of a prevailing myth that the whole area of psychological disturbance can be rendered "objective" and "scientific" when in fact it is much more of a personal art form. While the increasing dominance of a pharmacological approach may seem to be the way of all scientific medicine, the treatment of human persons in a most intimate of ailments may require something more elusive than science, namely wisdom and a capacity to discern the inner motions of a person's spirit.

DELIVERANCE!

After the devastating events of my Sydney years, my life took a more steady course. I returned to the state of my birth and patiently rebuilt my life. I was once again able to take time at the farm. After several years of living alone, I welcomed a new partner into my life in 2008, and — miraculously in terms of what had preceded — was offered a faculty position as the inaugural Director of Lay and Continuing Education for the West Australian Synod of the Uniting Church. I now had a bunch of colleagues and a role I relished within the life of the church I had grown to love. The stressors of Sydney days were far removed, and I took up a new period of teaching and learning as a theological educator. I filled this position for seven years and then took up a part time lectureship in Homiletics and Missiology in the Perth Theological Hall.

In 2015, I retired from my career. It was towards the end of this year that I bought a small valve radio, housed in a warm, brown Bakelite cabinet. I had for years been looking for such a wireless, but they seemed to be no longer featured in junk shops and antique stores. Finally, I found an enthusiast who had several on sale at the craft fair to which my wife had dragged me along. Turning this set on, I waited for the valves to warm up and then I heard the familiar fifty cycle hum in the small loud speaker and then the sweet tones of a music program. I cannot describe adequately the joy this simple purchase afforded me. I could turn it on at any time and listen to music, or the summer cricket games, or even catch one of my favourite news programs. Of course, I had transistors, TV and audio equipment in the house. But a Bakelite valve radio that worked! Wow.

There was no miracle, of course. Radios had been available like this since the 1930s and here it was into the second decade of a new millennium. But for me joy was in this! I tried to reason why. Did it reconnect me with my fifteen-year-old self, when I played with valve radios as a hobby? Did it offer some sense of reclaiming items now deemed useless, rendering them once again useful? A conservationist's satisfaction? No, none of it worked to provide the answer. There seemed to be no justification for it at all! I just loved this little brown wireless. Wonderful! So, I bought two more sets — these ones not functional — and I set to work to find and correct their faults. Soon I had three or four of the old valve radios, all pumping out sweet sounds to my attuned ear. Perhaps there was a business opportunity here, radio repair in an age that believes rather in the "throw-away' philosophy.

But no, there was little money to be made in this way. And anyway, that is entirely besides the point. The point of this exercise, it seems, is that there is no point, that some things in life just bring joy, joy without reason, joy without utility. It then dawned on me that joy needs no justification; it is its own reason. And just as joy had suddenly disappeared from my life when I was a young teenaged boy, joy returned to this old man. For the moment, it seemed the circle had been made complete. I could not reason my way to joy, nor massage my ego to receive joy. One day it just came. And for that I thank God.

Of course, such highs fade in time. But as I took stock of my life, I saw that besides my complement of small radios, there was the farm, the good brown earth, my new marriage, and a family that grew as grand-children were born to my daughters. And beyond these wonderful blessings, there is the sense that I live in a world that is blessed by a good and loving God. Happiness rises and falls with the daily temperature and with the motions of the soul, but joy — simple, solid joy — now emerged as the fruit of my years.

6: SPIRITUALITY AND DEPRESSION

A CHEMICAL IMBALANCE?

We have now traced the arc of a lifetime engagement with depressive illness, one which included a descent into darkness as a teenaged boy and went on to encounter various types of treatment, concluding with an almost miraculous return of joy. It has been a tale of loss and recovery, of abandonment and deliverance, of an emerging maturity of understanding and prayerfulness. In this chapter, I wish to draw the threads together by asking what have we learnt about the nature of depression and its treatment.

In the course of this memoir, we have also traced developments in the medical treatment of depression over the last sixty years and noted the great advances made in the understanding of the pharmacology of depression. I have been a grateful beneficiary of these advances and do not wish in any way to detract from the great benefit these advances have brought to so many people. However, I wish to sound a cautionary note, and to suggest that there are dangers in the medicalisation of this condition, especially where it is not supported by a fully developed understanding of the human person and the nature of the illness.

I have hinted at the ways in which the "medicalisation" of the understanding of depression introduced certain biases and distortions into the treatment of depressed persons, with myself as a principal exemplar. To have offered this critique poses implicitly a much larger question. What is the nature of depressive illness and how is it related to a full understanding of the nature of the human person? Further, if scientific medicine — with its reliance upon pharmacology — falls short in its definition and understanding of the condition, is there a better framework in which to set the various findings and insights we have generated over the last generation or so?

Let us revisit a couple of key experiences. In being treated for bipolar, I experienced one aspect of the medical model, as a condition was diagnosed and a treatment mandated which caused great distress and no improvement of my condition. With scant attention to my reported experiences of the medications, my physicians worked from the diagnosis to what they believed was the best cocktail of drugs. It was as if my depression were being treated as an imbalance in brain chemistry and, once that was solved, the issue was dealt with. It took several weeks of adverse reaction before the approach to the meds was fundamentally rethought. Throughout the experience, I felt as if I were being treated as a biochemical machine, rather than a human person with feelings and desires and needs.

In time, of course, the treatment was corrected. I do not wish to dwell on the mistakes that often arise in the treatment of a complex illness, but only to use the incident to highlight the bias which the lack of a fully orbed definition of my condition and an understanding of my person introduced into the treatment and the patient experience. In this experience of treatment, the attention of the physicians was directed almost exclusively at the effect of the medications, and there was never time to discuss what was happening with my own psychological processes or my sense of personal direction. Theory rather than personal knowledge of the patient was allowed to determine the course of treatment, with the focus being almost exclusively upon the adjustment of medication

Of course, not all psychiatrists would be as singularly focused on pharmacology, but I was consulting with some of the top practitioners in the country, and expected that they knew what they were doing. No doubt, if asked, they would have claimed to be agnostic when it comes to the model or theory of the human person with which they were working. But in the absence of such a clear theoretical framework, the influence of popular models — such as the chemical imbalance idea — tend to shape their actions.

Take another example. It is well known that the best clinical practice for treatment of depression calls for a combination of medical/pharmacological and the personal/interpersonal aspects. It is commonplace to insist that one cannot proceed without the other. Yet, there is no model of the human person and of the actual condition being treated which enables us to unify these disparate treatment methodologies. Medical theory tends to proceed with notions of the mechanical body which is somehow inhabited by the psyche or person, rather like the proverbial "ghost in the machine". Of course, if we regard the machine as a "biochemical entity", then we have something of a model of the human person. But this is a remarkably crude model for understanding the human person, and no one would give it serious philosophical or psychological credence. In no way does it assist us to see why and how pharmacology and interpersonal therapy should cohere in the treatment of human persons. Yet in the absence of a more appropriate model, this model tends to provide a working rationale for treatment plans. Clearly, there is need for a better theoretical model of the human person and the particular pathology known as depressive illness.

THE DARK NIGHT OF THE SOUL

If we turn to a very different tradition, we find an alternative engagement with many of symptoms featured in our discussion. The sixteenth century mystical writer, St John of the Cross, describes in detail the mystical experience of the "dark night of the soul".[10] In many ways, what he has written parallels our account of the experience of depression, although there are important differences too. On the one hand, he speaks of a loss of "consolations" of prayer, by which he means that the usual pleasure and fulfilment one might gain from an act of prayer seems to go missing. Other practices that usually bring joy and satisfaction cease to do so, and generally the person lacks the motivation that usually drives them to prayer. This loss of joy and motivation speak of conditions we are familiar with from our discussion of depression. Rather than place these experience in the context of medical pathology, John sees the "dark night" as a normal and integral part of the soul's ascent to union with God.

In this framework, the experiences point not to a pathology in the person, but to a difficult truth about the way in which God works in the human soul, namely that it is "obscurely" or "in darkness". Indeed, the darkness is to protect the soul from too close an approach to God's mystery. In the dark night of the soul, the person is encouraged to persevere until the consolations return in due course. Not only will they return, but the person who has traversed this "dark night" will now see the presence and working of God in a new light. The separation between God and the rest of creation begins to dissolve, and the person is given a new freedom to love and serve the creation, as God loves and serves it. The movement begins to occur in a person, where the active work of meditation becomes more like the simple gift of contemplation.

Thus, the experience of the dark night, the loss of consolation and desire, are actually signs that God is working in the soul in deeper albeit obscure ways. While the soul may feel abandoned by God, in actuality, the experience really signifies that God's work within a person is proceeding to new and deeper levels. No doubt, for John's readers, this teaching posed a great encouragement to persist in the spiritual life and in the quest to find deeper union with the divine. While we may doubt that this insight would be of much assistance to a contemporary person suffering depression, it may help us to discern new ways of understanding that experience.

I believe it would be helpful to think of the experience of depression as the sign of development of a new level of consciousness, both of the self and of the wider world. It is an experience that makes naïve beliefs drop away, and can certainly leave one shaken and without any secure foundation in self- understanding and confidence in the trustworthiness of the world. But it is not necessarily so. As John saw so clearly, it is possible to grow beyond this point, to experience a new depth of awareness and self- command. If depression is put in the framework of spiritual growth rather than pathology, we are in a position to grasp these positive outcomes more definitely. This would be just one advantage of a new framing of this common experience.

Are there further points where John's analysis could shed light on our modern dilemmas? According to John, the human soul is motivated by its desire for union with God. The soul of a person is comprised both of a sensory aspect and a spiritual aspect. The first relates to our senses, and the second to our intellect, will and memory. In the "dark night of the soul", the enjoyment of these capacities is dulled, and the motivation of the soul drops away. This certainly accords with our account of the experience of depression in that a depressed person finds prayer a pointless exercise, and all motivation seems to be lacking.

Whether or not we buy into the medieval psychology, let alone the theological assumptions employed by John, the proposal that the mind of a person has both sensory elements and "higher" or spiritual elements seems to hold. If the disruption that we call depression means a displacement or disarraying of these capabilities, the implication is that setting this matter to rights will involve the whole person in a move towards reintegration and re-ordering. That there might be physical/pharmacological aspects as well as higher mental or spiritual aspects would be an obvious implication. Might it be helpful, then, to regard depression and or mood disorders as fundamentally disturbances of a person's spirit, and to propose that the treatment of them should be a form of holistic therapy that embraces body, mind and spirit?[11]

Perhaps we may state it in the follow way: for the depressed person, prayer as a plea for the darkness to lift seems far-fetched and is not to be encouraged. It promotes a kind of magical thinking that can have the effect of deepening the sense of doom when there is no sudden answer or relief of symptoms. But prayer as the kind of waiting in hope for a change in the weather of the soul is another matter altogether. This kind of prayer, it seems to me, has real possibility as being a useful and even therapeutic habit for the person, man or woman, who is experiencing the darkness of the absence of God.

A further implication relates to the experience of mania. If depression is understood as a profound disfigurement of a person's spirit, then it is all the more true of the condition during a manic episode. Here, one seems to lose contact in a very fundamental way with one's own spirit. If prayerfulness seemed to have dropped out of my life in the months leading up to my manic episode, then it is certainly the case that during this episode the quieter disciplines of prayer dropped out of my life altogether. This does not mean that I ceased to believe in God, or that God somehow withdrew from me, Simply, I was not present to God.

Faced with the unsatisfactory alternatives of "a chemical imbalance in the brain" or a "dark night of the soul", we might then pose a third possibility: a spiritual disturbance. Clearly, it is beyond the scope of this brief memoir to fully develop the arguments for such a definition; still we might draw together the threads of this narrative in this way. It seems to me that viewing these mood disorders as a spiritual disfigurement offers a way to hold together the important medical insights with a wider vision of what it is to be a healthy human person.[12] If a person suffers a profound spiritual disfigurement, then it stands to reason that prayer and any sense of the loving presence of God would become problematic.

Further, therapy would be directed towards assisting the person suffering this spiritual disfiguration to find their way back into a sustaining network of relationships. Isolation would be contra-indicated, and the careful development of a set of relationships which fully acknowledge the present suffering and limitation of the patient would be paramount. In part, the work of the counsellor or therapist must be to assist the person once again to sing their own song, to recognise their own voice when that very voice has been silenced. The role of conversation and mutual recognition is fundamental.

The proposal that depression be regarded as spiritual disfigurement points to the holistic nature of the treatment, which will usually include psychotropic medications, but can never be limited to these. In the process of treatment and recovery, the person would be encouraged to pick up the spiritual narrative of their lives and to reintegrate themselves and this latest experience into that on-going story. Nothing less than the engagement with the whole person and their reintegration into a network of relationships — and not merely with the medical profession! — including their sense of the exercise of their eclipsed spiritual capacities, can suffice as a treatment model for patients suffering this kind of disorder. [13]

My memoir is ended but I wish to highlight now what happened to me as I stood on the banks of the Murrumbidgee River.

EPILOGUE

It's today or never, I concluded. If I don't cross the river today, I'll probably never again be given the opportunity. The year was 1995 and I had come to this place to make a retreat. Towards the end of the year, I knew I was facing an emotional and spiritual crisis. I had made a successful transition into pastoral ministry, had achieved a major reform of the local congregations and was well-regarded by my parishioners. Yet during the year I had applied for two academic positions and although short-listed and interviewed, I was passed over for the positions. I was beginning to feel trapped in my parish work. Besides that, I was feeling exhausted and without spiritual resource. It was a classic case of "burnout"! One afternoon, my wife and I met with a Spiritual Director, Revd Ross Kingham, and I told him of my condition. Rather than send me to my GP or psychiatrist, Ross told me I needed to make a retreat.

Two weeks later, I was on retreat outside of Canberra. On the first day, I wrote:

What of my life? If I were to sum it up in one word that word would be "pressure". Pressure, pressure, pressure. There always seems to be pressure. Even when I go to the farm, there is a certain pressure to "get things done". Dad applies the pressure, in part, even last Friday he asked. "Well, what can we do now that we are here?" And it it's not Dad, it's me. Get something done.

Ross directed me to consider Isaiah 55 and let it guide my reflection and prayer. In my laptop I noted that in this text there was a list of imperatives starkly at odds with the imperatives that caused me so much pressure in my life. I listed them:

come to the waters… come, buy and eat…
listen carefully to me, and eat what is good,
and delight yourselves in rich food
incline your ear and come to me;
listen, so that you may live…
See… see…
Seek the Lord… call upon him…
let the wicked forsake their way
and the unrighteous their thoughts;
let them return to the Lord…

This list of imperatives picks up my sense of demands. I live my life under the pressure of demands that come to me, "Do this, do that, achieve this, excel at that, hurry for the time is short, and you might miss one of the tasks". My demands are for action, for achievement, to satisfy or mollify my elders, meet the wishes of those who depend upon me.

Yet Isaiah's group of imperatives are of a quite different kind. In a sense, they are more passive. They urge the hearer to nourish him- or herself, not to spend oneself in nourishing others. They call me to be quiet and listen, to notice the activity of another. I am to seek the Lord while he may be found. That is certainly a different direction from the demands that shape my life! I was making headway.

I came stuck, however, when I encountered the final part of the text.

For you shall go out in joy
and be led back in peace;
the mountains and the hills before you
shall burst into song,
and all the trees of the field shall clap their hands.
Instead of the thorn shall come up the cypress
instead of the brier shall come up the myrtle;
and it shall be to the Lord for a memorial,
for an everlasting sign that shall not be cut off.

Beautiful and compelling though these words were, they did not speak of my experience. I tried rewriting them to conform them more to my circumstances.

For you shall leave the place of bondage and depression in joy.
Not manic release, but solid joy of the heart.
The very places of your life, the city with its streets and
buildings,the farm with its hills and dales
shall reflect your joy and celebrate with you.
No longer sombre places, hard streets, places of loneliness,
they shall resound with the litany of joy.
Things will grow again, the ground of your life become fertile,
not things that wound your spirit and pierce your skin
but things that speak of beauty and the craft of excellence,
of quality, of satisfaction.
These things will be like a building that stands secure,
not a whim, a passing mood, a folly, a seven-day wonder,
no anxious high, giving vertigo and overlaying fear.
But a sign of everlasting love and mercy and goodness,
the Joy of the Lord.
Still my response was to reject.
Oh yeah, tell me another one!!
It's all been promised before, and it has never delivered.

I wrote, "It seems to me that my heart does not believe in joy, in joy as an everlasting memorial. It believes that sorrow is stronger and more reliable. The child in me, the little defenseless one, wants to believe, but he is shouted down by the louder voice, the voice of authority".

Ross suggested that there was something in my background unresolved, not confessed or forgiven. I reflected that, Yes, I am invited to partake of the joy and wholeness offered by God. In the great story of the Banquet, I am not one of the poor, the crippled, the blind and the lame. Yet still I am one of those who is stuck in a position where he is not able to taste of the fullness of the Lord. Often, I am able to help people with the issues of their lives, to offer support, encouragement, add words of wisdom. But I cannot tell them how to live their lives, because deep down I don't really know how to live mine. I know how to get along, but the way seems to involve so much pain and discouragement at the moment that I dare not recommend to others that you follow in my way.

Not that my prayer life is all that great. It's just at a beginning point, which this issue suggests. How can I affirm that God is beyond the sense of sight? How should he come to me if I were blind or deaf? Or if my emotions were so disordered that I could no longer feel the exultation of God's grace, or the peace of God deep within my soul? How then would I know God/how pray to God? It may well be that I am in a disordered state of emotion — depression highlights the dark, saps the joy, renders one without energy.

Ross introduced the Jungian perspective that holds that the task of the second half of life is to integrate the shadow side of ourselves. I was familiar with this view from earlier reading, but it seems it would be advantageous to think more directly about the shadow side. This reflection and a recent experience of my father's critical voice led me to the insight that my father stood to me both as supporter and critic. My critical voice, trained to a knife edge in my academic career, was very strong within my psyche. Combined with my perfectionist tendencies, this force was a powerful determinant of my personality. On this retreat, I was learning to take on the critic rather than simply giving in to his fierce-sounding advances. But it was something of an intellectual victory; it didn't break through into real conscious experience until I swam the Murrumbidgee River that snakes through this rural property.

On the second last day of the retreat, I decided to confront the river. Walking away from the farm-house, along the fields and down the old four-wheel drive track, my mind was anxious — fretting over the deal I had made to purchase a computer which seemed to be going wrong. I told God it wasn't all that important. Yeah, only $2000 in the accounts of a strapped Minister of Religion. Still, Lord, it's not worth worrying about. Then why am I so fearful? Lack of faith, I guess. No, that's not it. Your Dad was a panic artist, remember. Not a lot of confidence in his judgment or the peaceable nature of the Kingdom. Perhaps it's just the way you are. Perhaps you ought to know that, and not make risky gambits when you are trying to focus, to pray, to retreat. You tend to pack your life with many unnecessary hassles, you know. Yes, I know.

As I came to the river bank and the large black rocks that line it, I saw my old friend, the four-legged lizard. It was his rock, he said. Shot his tongue out at me. Well, I'm sorry, matie, but today I am going to occupy this rock with you. It's warm here out of the breeze, in the sunlight, and I need this warmth as much as you do. Not likely, he seemed to say, and then he took up his post, guarding the rock from any further incursion of this big flabby white thing. I took my clothes off, and stretched out in the sun, glorious it was, and the river streamed past us, and I thought again of the nature of the creator of all this. I was still trying to drive from my mind the anxiety about my foolish purchase.

It's today or never, I concluded. If I don't cross the river today, I'll probably never again be given the opportunity. But the current seemed strong, and the water was cold on my bare toes. Looking across the other side, I could see a beautiful waterfall playing over the rocks, and the suggestion of deep rock pools, higher up the hillside. I waded out into the water. I could feel the strength of the current now. The stream quickly got much deeper. I came back and reconsidered. Then I broke off a long stick, I waded out a second time, checking the depth of the water in front of me. I was nearly swept off my feet in the downward sloping bottom, nearly lost my stick and dropped my shoes in the water. Back again. Well, I'll have to swim it, which means leaving my shoes and my glasses back here. I'll just have to half-see it all and scramble over the rocks with my tender bare feet.

I had to make a decision, one way or the other. Wading out as far as I could, I launched myself into the deep, cold rapidly moving water. As it grabbed hold of me, my arms sprang into motion and found myself swimming as strongly as possible. I was moving rapidly, both downstream and across, and in next to no time I felt the sandy bank under my feet. Rising up out of the water I exulted. Made it! I clambered over the strewn rocks as carefully as I could. Came upon the beautifully limpid rock pool at the foot of the waterfall. Here the rock shelved back towards the pool in a large flat area. It was sunlit as I stretched myself out on the warm rock to dry. I felt like a kid again.

Are you proud of me, Mum, the way I swam that unknown river and now camp like a wild man on this rock ledge?

You are my one, the Beloved: with you I am well pleased.

I bathed in the warm sunlight, accepting this word of approval. But there was more.

I accept the anxiety that chokes you. I accept the dark tired persona you carry. And I love the little one who dreams and hopes and enjoys all things, especially all the things in my creation. Especially him do I love. And though you are like the poor form of a man, rent down the middle with the sides of your person rubbing together in uneasy opposition, I know what you are, what it is like for you. It's that you I love, the disabled one.

No, I haven't heard God say that to me. It just came into my head. But I came close to hearing it on this retreat. I saw the loveable child, ran to meet him and put on him the finest robe, brought out the fatted calf, for him. Of course, the elder brother was lurking around, quite sulky and cranky he was. "I'll get you for this. Just you wait. When you're on the plane, or in bed with your wife, or once you take up parish duties again. I'll get you, don't you worry about that, you filthy little jerk."

I drew myself back and directed a rather plaintive prayer to God. "Oh Lord, what's to become of me?" The words that came were, "It's all right. He can't harm you in any way. I can handle him". My response, "Ah yes, Lord. So be it". Standing on the rock ledge, I sang till my lungs were ready to burst. "I'll praise my Maker, while I've breath. Jesu Lover of my soul, let me to thy bosom fly, while the nearer waters roll... spring thou up within my heart."

The following morning, I sought to write about my Shadow, the dark critic who seems to dog my steps and sap away my joy. I discovered that my Shadow was filled with light and it is me, the persona, who is full of darkness. This turned much of my thinking upon its head. If I have become the dark critic, it is because I have rejected the light of the child. My sin is not that I am depressed, but that I have not had the faith to trust in God, to accept the deep deep love of Jesus for the vulnerable child of the light.

This persona has separated herself from the hopes and dreams and joys and fears of this little one because she thinks they are too much to bear. In the course of being practical, she has well-nigh killed the genius that lurks in that child. If all this is right, then it is my persona that needs reforming, and not my shadow.

It was as if the "kind of adult" I have become after my first depressive episode (see chapter 1 above) was actually a pseudo-adult, which now needed to be discarded. It seemed that the real adult could only emerge as I abandoned this early attempt at adulthood and embraced instead the child, as it were, the truly "grown-up" child/adult I could become. My persona must be reformed in such a way that she values and nurtures this child side.

In past months, I had asked myself, "Why do I abuse myself so much? Why is there so much pain? Why do I pray to God to take my life? Why must I dwell in darkness all my livelong days?" The answer would appear to be that I am rejecting this hurriedly constructed ego for the sake of my adult emerging self. If this is so, then my joy, my self, my authority lies in the freeing of this little one and his integration into my adult ego. It seemed I was talking about a new kind of conversion. This healing of the self is what it means to be converted to God and can only be to draw near to one's truest joy.

APPENDIX: LIVING WITH THE BLACK DOG

GUIDELINES FOR SELF-TALK

During the disaster of my manic episode, a cluster of devastating events occurred, including the death of my father, the loss of employment and break-up of my marriage. Following these events, I entered a period of intense psychiatric treatment, checking myself into a Mood Disorder Unit. In many ways, this marked a new phase in my learning about depression and manic depression and from it I drew many important lessons.

In the psychiatric unit of the Clinic, I encountered many severely depressed patients, and others who were "higher than kites". I saw the effect on these folk of intensive medication therapy and electro-convulsive therapy (ECT). It became clear that my difficulties did not match these in intensity and that, in my case, rational faculties still operated, albeit at times distorted by the swings of my moods. The policy of the clinic was clear: gross mood disorders needed to be treated by medication at an appropriate level, often higher than people had previously been using. If this treatment did not alleviate a severe depression, some persons benefitted by ECT. The effectiveness of this time-tested treatment was quite remarkable to observe. Once an alleviation of the excesses of the mood had been treated, people were often ready to join an ongoing therapy group, where some of the milder forms of psychotherapy, such as Cognitive Behaviour Therapy (CBT) could be tried. I was soon sent on to this group.

Cognitive Behaviour Therapy on its own sometimes looks simplistic, as if its message is simply to accentuate the positive and attenuate the negative. In these terms, it seems to the depressed person like a kind of "Pollyanna" therapy. However, if we think of it in terms of the polarity within the self between the self-nurturing aspect and the self-denigrating aspect, it makes more sense. In a depressed frame of mind, the self-denigration holds upper sway, and this goes to the heart of the problem. In the therapy group, from the beginning, I was put in touch with my self-nurturing capacity, emerging from the tone set by the two psychologists who supervised the group. They consistently pointed to the self-nurturing aspect of the experiences of group members and encouraged us to avoid self-denigration and self-flagellation. While affirming our pain and the difficulties of our struggle, they maintained an objectivity that pointed towards the more practical and constructive ways of dealing with feelings, issues, people and situations.

It might be useful to the reader if I now listed some of my discoveries while engaging in this process, and indeed throughout the memoir that has preceded. Rather than give a series of third person instructions — which would be far too didactic for this memoir — I would like to list them in the mode of "self-talk", the kind of rules which I have come to urge upon myself, in good times and in bad. Regard the following, then, as a check-list of self-talk, directions it might at times be helpful to follow.

You are your own worst enemy: you need to become your own best friend.

The sense of solidarity and companionship of the group was very important to me. I found there is a special bond among people who suffer depression. In all my time, both in the Mood Disorder Unit and the Group, I never heard a depressed person respond inappropriately to another. Sometimes "outsiders" can respond in ways that are unhelpful or inappropriate, but there is a kind of solidarity among those who know it from the inside, and this in large part enables the self-nurturing capacity we all possess. My second learning then:

Only you know the magnitude of your depression: the solidarity of others who suffer similarly is a great source of encouragement.

Cognitive Behaviour Therapy added a new tool to my bag of tricks. It is a very practical tool that doesn't seek to solve the problems of life or find the causes of my depression. Rather, it encourages active and intentional change in cognitive behaviour by giving attention to such factors as the following:

- Depression encourages me to have negative thoughts and these, in turn, deepen my depression. Therefore, it is important to call a halt, invent a "circuit breaker", become aware of negative thoughts and as far as possible consciously replace them with positive thoughts, by whatever means you can devise.

- Depression makes me want to be passive, and passivity makes me feel worse about myself. Thus, passivity sets a kind of trap. Therefore, in manageable doses, seek to engage in helpful activity, especially physical activity.

- Perfectionism makes one believe that unless what one does is done perfectly, it is better to do nothing. But this leads into the trap of passivity, mentioned above. Therefore, it is important to try to break down the expectation of a perfect performance and to mark and celebrate modest achievements.

- Depression causes you to compare your performance unfavourably with others who are seen to be closer to perfection than you are. It is a no-win situation, so take care to avoid all comparisons. (No one said this would be easy!)

To summarise these into a third learning:

> **Mind and body are integral to mood. Mental hygiene is as important as physical hygiene when you are depressed. You cannot help the way you feel, but you can make other plans — and carry them out!**

Depression leads one to be preoccupied with one's own feelings and problems. This preoccupation is not part of the reality of those others among whom we move. That is, an issue is looming large in our minds, but it is an issue that does not arise for others! There is a kind of focus on something which is not really an issue at all. If we realise this, we can save ourselves the grief of projecting our negative feelings and negative judgments about ourselves onto others. (Again, not easy to achieve!) In a strictly logical sense, our own preoccupations do not occur to others. In some ways, the mental state of depression can be defined as follows.

> **You are preoccupied with an issue that does not arise: seek some other focus.**

Relationships in the group were sustaining and the experience led me to seek to find that in other relationships. On the one hand, it is easy to get into the wrong relationships that only deepen the depression: on the other hand, it is not difficult to reach a position where depression has poisoned a good relationship. This is difficult but must be faced. We cannot expect everyone to understand or empathise with our experience or to know how best to relate to it. But we can seek out helpful relationships, avoid destructive and unhelpful ones. It is important to communicate with clear signals to those who love us. It is possible to enter a committed love relationship along the way before we are "cured" or otherwise made perfect! The single life is not to be despised: it is possible to survive alone with the right network of friends.

The role of the other is vital in living with depression: choosing the other must be done with care and wisdom.

Finally, we can address ourselves to the "best friend" self, which I also call "beloved".

So, beloved…

There is no magic bullet for depression. We need many tools in our bag of tricks. When it is ready, when you are ready, depression will recede. You will not miss it. What you have learnt may have the effect of reshaping the rest of your life.

SPIRITUAL PRACTICE

The self-talk proposals in the previous section were worked out in the context of a secular institution and secular processes. But let us now feed into them the insights of the previous chapter in which depression was regarded as a spiritual disfiguring of the human person. It is possible to revisit each of these learnings with a view to their expansion into the spiritual reality we have insisted properly belongs in the discussion of depression. As we now revisit these learnings, we set them alongside what we may learn about the spiritual journey.

First Message

**You are your own worst enemy: you need to become your
own best friend.**

As we have suggested throughout this memoir, it is precisely at this
point that prayer become problematic. For the person suffering mild
to severe depression, the sense of a benign presence rudely vanishes.
Prayer becomes a form of self-talk which is all the more unhelpful
because the self we seem to talk most easily to is the "worst enemy"
self. If one were able simply as an exercise of will to summon up the
"best friend" self, then it might well be that prayer would begin to
"work" again. But this is easier said than done.

The fundamental datum of most Christian theology is that "God
is love". In a healthy mental state, it is entirely sensible to make the
further bold claim that "God loves *me*." We see this most clearly in the
Psalms of David.

> The Lord is *my* shepherd
> *I* shall not want.
> He makes *me* lie down
> in green pastures,
> He leads *me* beside still waters…
>
> Even though *I* walk through the darkest valley
> *I* shall fear no evil
> for you are with *me*
> your rod and your staff – they comfort *me*. (Psalm 23)

The move from theology to personal experience is the one that the
depressed psyche seems incapable of making. The words can be heard,
but their application to the depressed person seems impossible.

As a consequence, no amount of reading or hearing the Psalms is
likely to bring about any relief of the symptoms of depression. Another
move is needed before they can be of any comfort. It seems it is only
as we access the "best friend" within our own selves that we can
encounter the "best friend" God. So how can we begin to make this
transition? We will return to this point in conclusion.

Second Message

Only you know the magnitude of your depression: the solidarity of others who suffer is a great source of encouragement.

The depressed person seeking fellowship in a Church will often come away feeling much worse. What he has encountered is a group of people who *appear* to be super happy and really super-achievers! Of course, the reality may well be otherwise, but everyone in the Church is probably putting on their "Sunday Best" when it comes to what they project and how they connect with others. The one who might seem to be a bit "down" is invariably slapped on the back and told to "cheer up!" My former wife used to advise me quite strongly when I was depressed not to go to Church! She knew the chances were it would only pitch me deeper in.

In terms of Christian history, it is useful to realise that what we today call "church" is a modern sociological construct. In the very different social reality of the early church, the meaning of the word ecclesia was simply that of a gathering of people. We learn from the letters of Paul that many of the "churches" met in homes. Perhaps they were more like what today we call "home groups". Certainly, in our terms they were comparatively "small groups", and bear no resemblance to modern day "congregations". But as the modern form of the congregation begins to pass away, it may well be that the home group movement points the way forward for a recovery of the sense of the *ecclesia*. Certainly, it is the case for the depressed person that the kind of "church" that can be useful is the home group or small group, where bonds of intimacy mean that the kinds of social pretense that can become normal in congregations fades out of currency.

In the context of this small group form of "church", the reality of one's mood can be shared without being "trumpeted from the rooftops". In addition, trust can be established to the point where members of the group know how to avoid the crasser forms of "positive thinking" mentality that so often prevails in other settings. I do not wish to idealise the small group: certainly, there are small groups in which no genuine trust or intimacy is achieved, and social pretense flourishes.

The point I wish to make is that for the one with the vulnerability of a depressed mood, groups need to be sought out in which it can be safe to be honest about feelings. Such a group can function as a community of support and encouragement to the one suffering the ups and downs of a mood disorder.

Indeed, we might be so bold as to say that such a group can begin to function as "the body of Christ". I wish to introduce this note because it is a fundamental of Christian theology that in the person of Jesus Christ God actually suffers, as we suffer. To understand that God in Christ is a fellow sufferer in the pains of life and death is a very powerful message, one that can be communicated by a real experience of the community as the body of Christ. The solidarity of other followers of Jesus in both the suffering of God and the suffering of the person who is mood disordered can actually work great changes.

Third Message

Mind and body are integral to mood. Mental hygiene is as important as physical hygiene when you are depressed. You cannot help the way you feel, but you can make other plans—and carry them out!

This point was developed out of engagement in Cognitive Behaviour Therapy or CBT. With its focus upon behaviour and cognition, this therapy is very concerned with mind and body and their integration. While useful for mildly depressed persons, it is not particularly useful for people with moderate to severe mood disorder. Its limitation lies in its reliance upon rational thinking and behaviour, which may be beyond the person with major mood issues. How does it relate to spiritual perspectives on living?

I have suggested in the previous chapter that depression is best understood as a disfigurement of the spirit. For there is more to personal life than mind and body; there is indeed a place where they meet, and what is that? Further, we find that unity of the person is something that endures through all the changes in body and mind to which we are subject in the normal processes of maturation and aging. This, I suggest, is the reality of spirit. With this perspective in mind, we might wish to expand this point in the following way.

Mind and body are integral to spirit, and mood is a linking between each of them. A healthy relationship between mind and body is a function of the spirit, although in mood disorders this relationship suffers degrees of distortion.

While it is true for the minimally functioning person that planning is possible, in the severely depressed even the act of planning — let alone the will to carry out a plan — seems to go missing. Accessing the self-nurturing capacities discussed earlier becomes almost impossible. To find one's way into a moment of spiritual awareness and uplift likewise is beyond capability. But as mood is moderated and mind and spirit begin to function again, it is possible for a person to find some joy in the fellowship of supportive others and even to be moved by the singing of beloved hymns and spiritual songs.

The spirit, so vulnerable to disorder in the mood disorder realm, is actually very robust in the long term. It is able to recover from the darkest night of the soul! Indeed, the spiritual literature regularly speaks of the journey into darkness as an element in spiritual training. Part of the spiritual journey is learning no longer to fear the darkness, which may be the darkness of mood disorder or simply the fading of a bright spiritual light. The actual robustness of the spirit enables persons — with suitable support and encouragement — to grow out of persistent darkness into something more like the light and shade of regular life.

Fourth Message

You are preoccupied with an issue that does not arise: seek some other focus.

Most depressed persons have the experience of being "somewhere else" from other folks. The preoccupations which the disorder engenders often lead to isolation and misunderstanding. While it is no use to be counselled to "snap out of it", the realisation that the issue with which one is preoccupied does not even occur to others can be liberating. It seems to me that we need to be able to tell ourselves this when the mood threatens. Yes, for the depressed person, issues of worth and competence may loom large, yet for the rest of the group or community they do not usually arise!

Here again the support of a loving faith community can work wonders. For a group to gently insist that they are not in the business of judging the saddened one but want to join with him or her in their suffering and enable the revival of self-nurturing gifts can be an act of real redemption. Here I think faith in a loving God, upheld by a loving faith community, can provide just the "other focus" which this learning calls forth. Indeed, as we are encouraged to stand before God, love and mercy may be experienced by the spirit that has known the loving support of the community.

Fifth Message

The role of the other is vital in living with depression; choosing the other must be done with care.

While depression can be experienced as terribly isolating, it can form the basis for new and more enriching relationships. But the care with which these relationships are chosen and formed is the key. It is a sad fact of human experience that some relationships become toxic and should be avoided. The connection between two people is a deeply spiritual matter, it's as if spirit speaks to spirit. When connection does not occur at this level, it may be that this is not a relationship worth preserving. Letting go is never easy, but sometimes a person must let go of a relationship to move on with their own progress towards health and wholeness. We want every friendship to be forever, but the truth of our lives is that moving on is more constant than staying put.

Encountering the Best Friend

At the end of my narrative, perhaps we can see it as a journey to discover my Best Friend. What can now be said about beginning and sustaining such a journey to the rediscovery of the joy of life? I believe our own capacity for love and self-regard can be recovered only through the friendship of others — we cannot do it alone. It begins with taking into one's confidence a faithful confident who is prepared to travel alongside. I am talking here about *professional* help. In the course of my journey, I have sought such professional assistance from General Practitioners, Psychiatrists, Counsellors, Pastoral Carers, Ministers and Spiritual Directors.

The professional plays a vital role in any journey out of depression, and I strongly urge those who avoid such a relationship to take note of this point. Your spouse, your parents, even a good mate, cannot serve the role of primary confidant in this pathway — they are too close; and, besides, these valued relationships have other functions in our lives. If you are serious about leaving depression behind, you need the balance and security that a professional relationship affords. The one seeking relief from a mood disorder must take responsibility for it and not think that they can simply hand it over to a spouse or parent. It is not fair to the other person, and can poison a perfectly good relationship, or else simply lead you down the pathways of co-dependency.

With each of the persons I have consulted, there has emerged a healing relationship. One counsellor saw his role as enabling me 'to sing again my own song'. Another taught me to re-tell the narrative of my life in ways that set me free from learned bondage. Whatever the methodology, each professional managed to identify my 'best friend self' and to point me towards him. From time to time, I am still prone to self-destructive ways, but increasingly I am able to recognise them for what they are and to turn back to the best friend I always need.

But 'professional help' is only a beginning point: one needs a whole network of friends and partners to see the journey through. Not all friendships endure; and many relationships, entered with great enthusiasm, have to be discarded, often with sorrow and regret. But the value of faithful partners, abiding friends and loving communities of support cannot be overstated. Each of them, in different ways, points to an undergirding of friendship that is the key to sustaining the journey to wholeness and joy.

There is, I believe, a friendship that is forever: the relationship with God or the ultimate ground of our being. I have stressed that there are times when this relationship seems far away and unthinkable but for the person in recovery, it is an ever-renewable possibility. I have discovered that there is an intimate connection between our experience of our 'best friend' self and our capacity to experience the friendship of God. In the light of our exploration of depression, it is helpful to consider God as the ultimate ground of our best friend self, the **source of best friending**. This might be the meaning of 'God is love'. God is the One whom we can know as the ultimate Beloved in life. The words are easily said but to experience that love in the dynamics of a life fully lived is a measure of good health. Such is the vision of wholeness with which this memoir can conclude. In such a friendship, not only is love experienced, joy too is recovered.

These words have been written in the conviction that healing and wholeness is a possibility for each of us, and that for the person suffering from a mood disorder, the journey towards that wholeness embraces the fullness and richness of our spiritual tradition. My proposal is that we take hold of this tradition more holistically and centrally in our understanding of both what ails us and what can bring us to the place of joy and peace. Wellness of spirit embraces all that we know about human reality, its biochemistry and its relationships, and out of these something deeper emerges, an inner sense of the divine presence, rich in trust and hope. The emergence of joy, like water from a hidden spring, tells us unfailingly of this healing Presence. May it be so for each of us.

Notes

1   It is very difficult to find words to describe this experience. Percy Knauth describes his first experience of depression, as an adult, as a "descent into hell". The image of hell is also used by Linda Thompson. Thompson speaks of "images of hell" as she struggles to articulate what was happening to her during a depressive episode. This is an experience which has a catastrophic and totalising impact, and language struggles to capture this. See Percy Knauth, *A Season in Hell* (Pocket Books, 1976), Linda E. Thompson, *Out of the Deep Blue* (Melbourne, ISBN 978-0-646-50514-5, 2008).

2   "Mood swing" is a term that came into the vocabulary with the work of Donald R. Fieve, who published his ground-breaking study in 1975. See Ronald R. Fieve, *Moodswing: The Third Revolution in Psychiatry* (Toronto, New York, London, Sydney: Bantam Books, 1976).

3   Sleep disturbance, especially with early anxious waking, is identified as one of the key markers of depression.

4   Linda Thompson speaks of her desire to suicide as present during most of her depressive episode. In her experience, the very perfecting of the suicide plan became an important, and in a strange way, therapeutic preoccupation. It was finally the discovery and resolution of a series of gastric issues that led to her release from both suicide and depression. For her, too, God disappeared from the landscape of reality. Indeed, it is only at the end of her journey that she can contemplate the possibility as she puts it, of piecing together "the few fragments of belief in God that remain".

5   Although the emotional disturbance of these early episodes was quite severe, I did not at any point consider taking time off from my work, except the temporary expedient of deferred examinations. It was very important to me that I "coped" with what was on my plate, and in a way, this perhaps preserved me from deeper disability. Linda Thompson also found that her work was important therapy in helping her to avoid the worst ravages of her illness, in her case, suicide. She writes, "Keeping my job was an essential survival strategy", Thompson, *Out of the Deep Blue*, p. 25.

6   A happy childhood seems to be no inoculation against the later onset of depression. Andrew Solomon, who has written extensively on his own experience of depression, reports his own early experiences as being very supportive. He writes, "I had a reasonably happy childhood with two parents who loved me generously, and a younger brother whom they also loved and with whom I generally got on well. It was a family sufficiently intact that I never even imagined a divorce or a real battle between my parents..." Andrew Solomon, *The Noonday Demon*, (London: Vintage, 2002) p. 39.

7   According to Andrew Solomon, "When it (depression) comes, it degrades one's self and ultimately eclipses the capacity to give or receive affection. It is the aloneness within us made manifest, and it destroys not only connection to others but also the ability to be peacefully alone with oneself.", Andrew Solomon, *The Noonday Demon*, p. 15

8   The correlation of the sense of self and the sense of God is well-known in the spiritual literature. For example, St Teresa of Avila reported to have heard God's voice in prayer saying, "Seek yourself in Me, and in yourself seek Me". Gerald G. May, *The Dark Night of the Soul: A Psychiatrist Explores the Connection Between Darkness and Spiritual Growth*, (New York: HarperSanFrancisco, 2004, p. 43. It stands to reason then that the kind of spiritual disturbance we are describing as depression should disturb both the relationship with self and with God, as well as with others. Linda Thompson speaks graphically of the experience of her depression as her own death at age 26 years. In this way, she points to the profound loss of her sense of herself as a feeling person.

9   Gerald May, reflecting on the writing of John of the Cross and Teresa of Avila, puts it in this way. "God is too intimate to be an object, too ultimate to be a thing...To our normal human capacities God is nada, "no-thing". Yet how easily in depression does this profound "no-thing" become a nothing!

10   I am indebted in what follows to the work of Gerald May. Gerald G. May, *The Dark Night of the Soul: A Psychiatrist Explores the Connection Between Darkness and Spiritual Growth*, New York: HarperSanFrancisco, 2004.

11   In important work on this theme, Larry Culliford proposes that a "spiritual history" should be part and parcel of any psychiatrist's initial engagement with a client. He argues that spiritual history is relevant in psychiatry for several reasons. First, the very nature of spirituality as a source of vitality, motivation and a healthy sense of belonging and being valued; second, the long historical relationship between religion, medicine and mental healthcare; third, the patient's needs and wishes; fourth, the epidemiology of spirituality/religion and mental health, fifth, the influence of spirituality/religion on the attitudes and decisions of psychiatric staff. The bringing together of spiritual dimensions with pathology points in a valuable direction for further exploration. Larry Culliford, "Taking a Spiritual History" in *Advances in Psychiatric Treatment* (2007), vol. 13, 212–219 doi: 10.1192/apt.bp.106.002774

12   See Tacey, D. (2006) Spirituality and the future of health. *Journal of the Scientific and Medical Network*, 91, 7 –10.

13   Culliford, L. (2002) Spiritual care and psychiatric treatment: an introduction. *Advances in Psychiatric Treatment*, 8, 249–258.